This journal belongs to:

_____

Quest 4
JOYFUL ABUNDANCE

Flow of the Alchemist...

Let it all flow...your dreams, your hopes, your innermost secrets for a magical Life.

At the end of Joyful Abundance, you will find your secret link and magic password to collect your surprise gift and your Quest 4 trophy.

Ignite
THE PATH TO A
MAGICAL LIFE

Start Date: _____

Completed: _____

Journal #: _____

Abundance goals for this month:

_____
_____
_____
_____
_____
_____
_____
_____

Abundance goals for this month:

Use this guided Abundance manifestation journal to...

- Boost positive thinking daily.
- Create juicy affirmations (Start them with "I am..." and use present tense).
- Journal and script your abundance journey as you desire! Some pages will be unlined, some will be lined. Each will have a gentle prompt related to Abundance.
- Share gratitude.
- Use the Doodle pages to write, contemplate and doodle free-form the way you love.
- Log all abundance you receive (rich experiences that cost nothing, expressions of love and kindness, gifts and money). If you run out of room, write on the Doodle pages.
- Enjoy light, consistent positivity by filling out 1-2 pages a day, or complete a chapter a day for an intensive 30-day experience...your choice!
- The page with the sun symbols are for mornings, the moon symbol for evenings. The journal and scripting pages can be done anytime but we recommend the mornings.

We will be using a unique version of the powerful Universal 3-6-9 numbering.

Enjoy the journey!

Notes & Doodles:

 Notes & Doodles:

 Abundance I already enjoy:

Live with the energy of abundance by focusing on it with:

- Frequency
- Consistency
- Simplicity

I live in a state of abundance!

My essence is abundant and free!

Each day, I immerse myself in the joy of ABUNDANCE!

6 Tips to Cultivate an Expansive Abundance Mindset:

1. Allow yourself to expand your possibilities and your potential, with gentleness and love.
2. Discover and brainstorm ways to add your extraordinary value to the world.
3. Take fearless steps forward on your creative ideas but focus on one at a time. Jump in with spirit and start!
4. Tweak with daring along the way. Don't be afraid to make a mistake but do listen to your intuition.
5. Appreciate all the signs of glorious abundance that come your way.
6. Master your daily money management like a boss so you can do the things you *love*.

My ideal abundant lifestyle:

My ideal abundant lifestyle:

Create a Morning High Vibe Routine:

My selections...

- ☐ Meditation
- ☐ Reading
- ☐ Exercising
- ☐ A Walk
- ☐ Journaling
- ☐ 10 minutes of anything fun

Other ideas:

_____
_____
_____
_____
_____
_____
_____
_____
_____

1

Abundance is first and foremost a state of being.

Abundance is primed from a state of mind and a state of emotion.

It allows you to see more about yourself, be yourself more, give more and receive more.

Let's visit your past BE-ing.

Date: _____

9 MINUTES OF SCRIPTING:
AMAZING THINGS YOU HAVE EXPERIENCED...

Date: _____

Your 3 favorite adventures:

Date: _____

WHAT ARE 3 WONDERFUL THINGS YOU RECEIVED IN THE PAST?

1 _____

2 _____

3 _____

WRITE 6 AFFIRMATIONS ABOUT ABUNDANCE (ANYTHING GOES)...

1 _____

2 _____

3 _____

4 _____

5 _____

6 _____

Scratch pad area...

Date: _____

LIST SOME THINGS YOU ARE SUPER GRATEFUL FOR TODAY!

ABUNDANCE LOG:
NOTE DOWN EVERYTHING YOU RECEIVED TODAY!

A world of creative abundance lives within you, waiting to be discovered.

JOYFUL LIFE MASTERY

2

Abundance is also about the flow - the process - with less focus on the end result.

Of course, the end result is desired and accomplishments are wonderful.

But it's your flow that sparks emotions and brings the magical element of attraction into your life!

Today's theme is based on the Flow of creation.

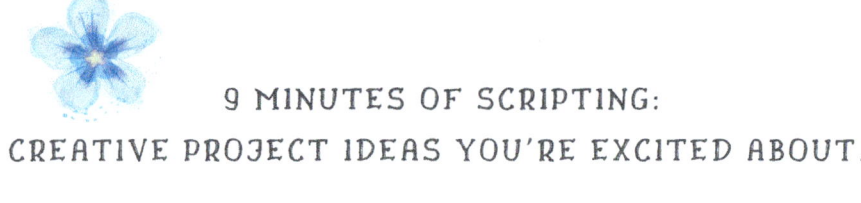

9 MINUTES OF SCRIPTING:
CREATIVE PROJECT IDEAS YOU'RE EXCITED ABOUT...

Your ideal abundant day:
Creating what you love...

Date: _____

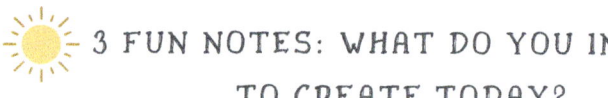 3 FUN NOTES: WHAT DO YOU INTEND
TO CREATE TODAY?

1 _____

2 _____

3 _____

WRITE 6 AFFIRMATIONS THAT DESCRIBE
WHAT YOU INTEND TO CREATE IN YOUR LIFE.

1 _____

2 _____

3 _____

4 _____

5 _____

6 _____

Scratch pad area...

Date

LIST SOME THINGS YOU ARE SUPER GRATEFUL FOR TODAY!

ABUNDANCE LOG:
NOTE DOWN EVERYTHING YOU RECEIVED TODAY!

"The key to abundance is meeting limited circumstances with unlimited thoughts."

Marianne Williamson

3

There must be space for Abundance to blossom, to grow, and to expand.

If our minds are full of mental clutter, it's difficult to attract abundant thoughts.

This theme is based on creating Space in the mental sphere.

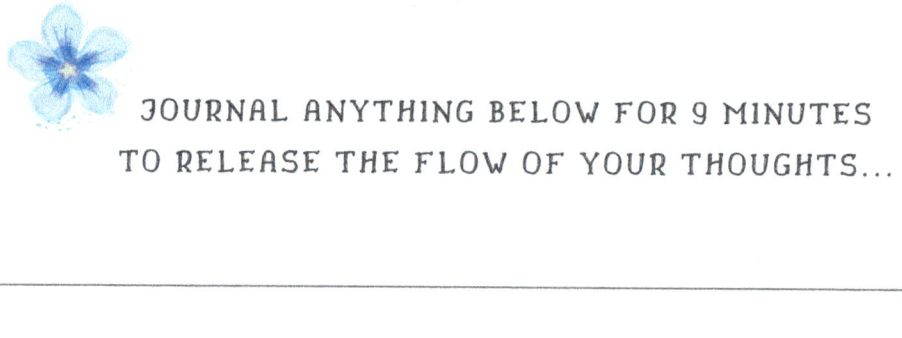

JOURNAL ANYTHING BELOW FOR 9 MINUTES
TO RELEASE THE FLOW OF YOUR THOUGHTS...

Your ideal abundant day:
At work...

Date: _____

 3 FUN NOTES: WHERE WILL YOU PUT YOUR FOCUS TODAY?

1. _____
2. _____
3. _____

CREATE 6 AFFIRMATIONS ON CLARITY AND FOCUS...

1. _____
2. _____
3. _____
4. _____
5. _____
6. _____

Scratch pad area...

Date

LIST SOME THINGS YOU ARE SUPER
GRATEFUL FOR TODAY!

_____
_____
_____
_____
_____
_____
_____

ABUNDANCE LOG:
NOTE DOWN EVERYTHING YOU RECEIVED TODAY!

_____
_____
_____
_____
_____
_____
_____
_____
_____

"Your fortune is not something to find but to unfold."

ERIC BUTTERWORTH

4

Inviting in more Abundance means being aware that it exists all around you now.

When you become aware of the Now within the flow of Life, you begin to understand in a deeply profound way, that the present moment is time unbound.

This theme is based on Presence.

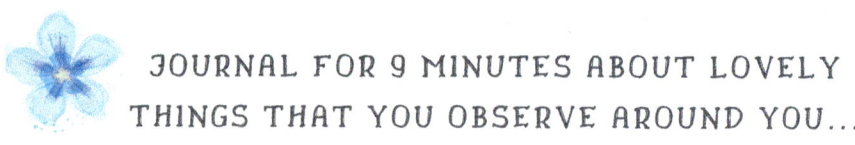

JOURNAL FOR 9 MINUTES ABOUT LOVELY THINGS THAT YOU OBSERVE AROUND YOU...

Your ideal abundant day:
At play...

Date: _____

 AS FAST AS POSSIBLE, NOTE DOWN WHAT YOU
WILL DO TODAY THAT FEEDS YOUR SOUL...

1 _____

2 _____

3 _____

AFFIRM 6 ASPECTS OF ABUNDANCE
IN YOUR LIFE RIGHT NOW...

1 _____

2 _____

3 _____

4 _____

5 _____

6 _____

Scratch pad area...

Date: _____

LIST SOME THINGS YOU ARE SUPER GRATEFUL FOR TODAY!

_____
_____
_____
_____
_____
_____
_____

ABUNDANCE LOG:
NOTE DOWN EVERYTHING YOU RECEIVED TODAY!

_____
_____
_____
_____
_____
_____
_____
_____

"Choose joyful abundance in your heart and be unbounded, free, and relaxed.
Be relentless with your choice and you'll make your mark."

Amy Leigh Mercree

5

The feeling of freedom rests at the core of the state of Abundance.

Freedom is an integral essence of Abundance. You have the freedom right now in this moment to decide what to consciously think about.

Today's theme is based on Freedom.

 JOURNAL FOR 9 MINUTES ABOUT ANYTHING YOU CHOOSE TO THINK ABOUT...

Your ideal abundant day:
Mornings...

Date: _____

 WHAT ARE 3 THINGS YOU'D LOVE TO THINK ABOUT TODAY?

1 _____

2 _____

3 _____

WRITE 6 AFFIRMATIONS OF YOUR CHOICE...

1 _____

2 _____

3 _____

4 _____

5 _____

6 _____

Scratch pad area...

Date

LIST SOME THINGS YOU ARE SUPER GRATEFUL FOR TODAY!

ABUNDANCE LOG:
NOTE DOWN EVERYTHING YOU RECEIVED TODAY!

When you realize there is nothing lacking, the whole world belongs to you.

LAO TZU

6

The energies of Abundance are freedom, expansiveness, generosity, optimism, joy, passion and happiness.

However, the great Secret is that these are not static states — they are found in the flow of Life.

Today's theme is based on the Abundant Energy of optimism.

 JOURNAL FOR 9 MINUTES ABOUT WHAT YOU LOOK FORWARD TO THE MOST THIS WEEK...

Your ideal abundant day:
Afternoons...

Date: _____

 WHAT ARE 3 THINGS YOU'RE REALLY
LOOKING FORWARD TO TODAY?

1 _____
2 _____
3 _____

AFFIRM HOW OPTIMISTIC YOU ARE
ABOUT 6 THINGS IN YOUR LIFE...

1 _____
2 _____
3 _____
4 _____
5 _____
6 _____

Scratch pad area...

Date: _____

LIST SOME THINGS YOU ARE SUPER GRATEFUL FOR TODAY!

_____
_____
_____
_____
_____
_____

ABUNDANCE LOG:
NOTE DOWN EVERYTHING YOU RECEIVED TODAY!

_____
_____
_____
_____
_____
_____
_____
_____

"The first step toward discarding a scarcity mentality involves giving thanks for everything that you have."

WAYNE DYER

7

Being in a state of Abundance means really enjoying all that you have around you...

Your home, your life, your loved ones - the beauty of Life's simple pleasures.

Today's theme is based on the Enjoyment of home.

FOR 9 MINUTES, JOURNAL WHAT ABUNDANCE LOOKS LIKE IN EVERY ROOM OF YOUR HOME...

Your ideal abundant day:
Home...

Date: _____

 PLAN 3 THINGS YOU ARE GOING TO
ENJOY IN YOUR HOME TODAY...

1 _____
2 _____
3 _____

WRITE 6 AFFIRMATIONS ABOUT
ABUNDANCE WITHIN YOUR HOME...

1 _____
2 _____
3 _____
4 _____
5 _____
6 _____

Scratch pad area...

Date:

LIST SOME THINGS YOU ARE SUPER
GRATEFUL FOR TODAY!

_____

_____

_____

_____

_____

_____

ABUNDANCE LOG:
NOTE DOWN EVERYTHING YOU RECEIVED TODAY!

_____

_____

_____

_____

_____

_____

_____

_____

"When we focus on our gratitude, the tide of disappointment goes out and the tide of love rushes in."

KRISTIN ARMSTRONG

8

Each 7 chapters, we will refresh the cycle.

We are revisiting Abundance as a state of being.

To energize Abundance in your life, celebrate the Abundance which already exists.

Today's theme is based on BE-ing in the present.

JOURNAL FOR 9 MINUTES ABOUT
HOW YOU FEEL TODAY AND WHY...

Your ideal abundant day:

Right here, right now. Script it out like a movie scene...

Date: _____

 WHAT ARE THE 3 BEST THINGS YOU
RECEIVED THIS WEEK?

1 _____

2 _____

3 _____

WHICH 6 PEOPLE DO YOU REALLY
APPRECIATE TODAY?

1 _____

2 _____

3 _____

4 _____

5 _____

6 _____

Scratch pad area...

Date: _____

LIST SOME THINGS YOU ARE SUPER GRATEFUL FOR TODAY!

_____
_____
_____
_____
_____
_____
_____

ABUNDANCE LOG:
NOTE DOWN EVERYTHING YOU RECEIVED TODAY!

_____
_____
_____
_____
_____
_____
_____
_____

Giving is the secret of abundance.

SIVANANDA

9

Today, we revisit the flow of Abundance.

When you give something away, whether it be a material gift or a non-material act of kindness, you naturally express your state of Abundance.

Today's theme is based on the Flow of giving.

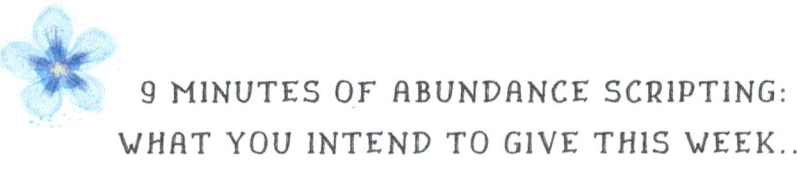

9 MINUTES OF ABUNDANCE SCRIPTING: WHAT YOU INTEND TO GIVE THIS WEEK...

Your ideal abundant week:
Evenings...

Date: _____

 3 FUN NOTES: WHAT DO YOU INTEND TO GIVE AWAY TODAY?

1 _____

2 _____

3 _____

DESCRIBE IN 6 AFFIRMATIONS HOW OR WHAT YOU LOVE TO GIVE...

1 _____

2 _____

3 _____

4 _____

5 _____

6 _____

Scratch pad area...

Date: _____

LIST SOME THINGS YOU ARE SUPER GRATEFUL FOR TODAY!

_____
_____
_____
_____
_____
_____
_____

ABUNDANCE LOG:
NOTE DOWN EVERYTHING YOU RECEIVED TODAY!

_____
_____
_____
_____
_____
_____
_____
_____
_____
_____

"What I know for sure is that when you declutter - whether it's on your home, your head, or your heart - it is astounding what will flow into that space that will enrich you, your life, and your family."

Peter Walsh

10

Today, we revisit the practice of making space for Abundance to grow.

To live in abundance manifest, ensure your current physical situation embodies the energy of abundance too.

Remove anything from your immediate area that embodies lack or hoarding. Surround yourself with things that make you feel abundant.

Today's theme is based on creating Space in the physical sphere.

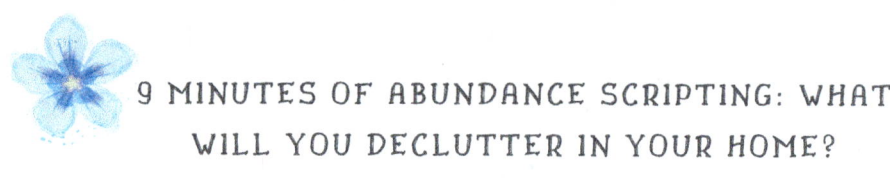

9 MINUTES OF ABUNDANCE SCRIPTING: WHAT WILL YOU DECLUTTER IN YOUR HOME?

Your ideal abundant week:
With lots of space...what will you put where?

Date: _____

 WHAT 3 ITEMS WILL YOU RELEASE FROM YOUR IMMEDIATE SPACE TODAY?

1. _____
2. _____
3. _____

WRITE AFFIRMATIONS ABOUT CREATING SPACE FOR 6 DIFFERENT TYPES OF ABUNDANCE...

1. _____
2. _____
3. _____
4. _____
5. _____
6. _____

Scratch pad area...

Date: _____

LIST SOME THINGS YOU ARE SUPER
GRATEFUL FOR TODAY!

_____
_____
_____
_____
_____
_____
_____
_____

ABUNDANCE LOG:
NOTE DOWN EVERYTHING YOU RECEIVED TODAY!

_____
_____
_____
_____
_____
_____
_____
_____
_____

"Any self-prompt that reminds you to focus on flow not ebb, contributes to your greater sense of abundance."

Sarah Breathnach

11

Abundance simmers in this moment's incredible potential. Mindfulness harnesses the power of presence.

Today's theme is based on mindful Presence.

9 MINUTES OF ABUNDANCE SCRIPTING: WHAT WERE YOUR MINDFUL EXPERIENCES YODAY AND HOW DID YOU FEEL?

Your ideal abundant week:
With your crafts and hobbies...

Date: _____

 WHICH 3 PRACTICES HELP YOU TO BE
MORE MINDFUL?

1 _____

2 _____

3 _____

AFFIRM 6 THINGS YOU REALLY
ENJOY ABOUT THESE PRACTICES...

1 _____

2 _____

3 _____

4 _____

5 _____

6 _____

Scratch pad area...

Date

LIST SOME THINGS YOU ARE SUPER GRATEFUL FOR TODAY!

ABUNDANCE LOG:
NOTE DOWN EVERYTHING YOU RECEIVED TODAY!

"And I said to my body softly, 'I want to be your friend.' It took a long breath and replied, 'I have been waiting my whole life for this.''

Nayyirah Waheed

12

Today, we revisit the feelings of freedom that rest at the core of Abundance.

Our bodies also need to feel free to be free. You are the only one who understands the ways in which your body expresses freedom.

Some people feel free when dancing, while some love running. For others freedom may be as simple as basking in the sunshine.

Today's theme is based on the Freedom of your body.

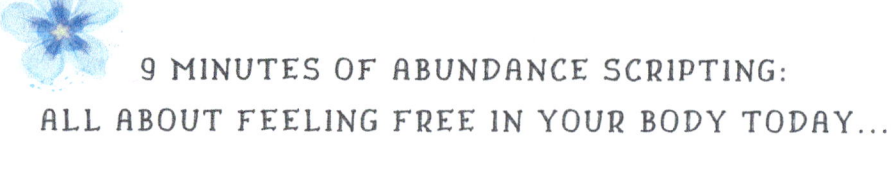

9 MINUTES OF ABUNDANCE SCRIPTING:
ALL ABOUT FEELING FREE IN YOUR BODY TODAY...

Your ideal abundant week:
Moving your body how you please...

Date: _____

 TODAY, INTEND TO DO 3 THINGS THAT WILL MAKE YOUR BODY FEEL JOYFULLY FREE...

1 _____
2 _____
3 _____

EXPRESS YOUR JOY AT BEING FREE IN YOUR BODY WITH 6 AFFIRMATIONS...

1 _____
2 _____
3 _____
4 _____
5 _____
6 _____

Scratch pad area...

Date:

LIST SOME THINGS YOU ARE SUPER GRATEFUL FOR TODAY!

ABUNDANCE LOG:
NOTE DOWN EVERYTHING YOU RECEIVED TODAY!

"If you carry joy in your heart, you can heal any moment."

CARLOS SANTANA

13

Today we revisit the beautiful energies of Abundance.

Your awareness of the flow of Life lights the spark of joy. When joy fills the present, allow it to expand into the next moment.

Today's theme is based on the Abundant Energy of joy.

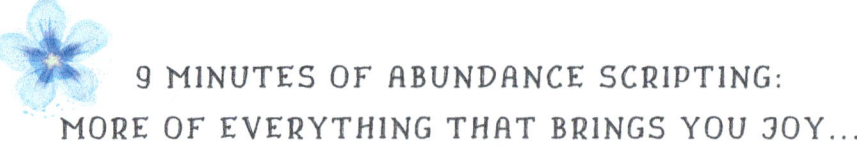

9 MINUTES OF ABUNDANCE SCRIPTING:
MORE OF EVERYTHING THAT BRINGS YOU JOY...

Your ideal abundant week:
With all the fun that you desire...

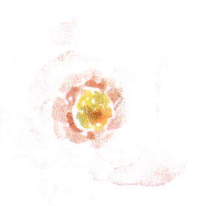

Date: _____

 WHAT ARE 3 THINGS THAT MAKE YOU
FEEL TRUE JOY?

1 _____

2 _____

3 _____

WRITE 6 AFFIRMATIONS CELEBRATING
WHAT YOU FIND JOYFUL IN YOUR LIFE...

1 _____

2 _____

3 _____

4 _____

5 _____

6 _____

Scratch pad area...

Date

LIST SOME THINGS YOU ARE SUPER
GRATEFUL FOR TODAY!

ABUNDANCE LOG:
NOTE DOWN EVERYTHING YOU RECEIVED TODAY!

"Find gratitude in the little things and your well of gratitude will never run dry."

ANTONIA MONTOYA

14

Today we revisit the Abundant state of enjoyment.

Let's celebrate the rich relationships of family (or whomever counts as family for you).

Today's theme is based on the Enjoyment of family.

9 MINUTES OF ABUNDANCE SCRIPTING: JOYFUL MEMORIES WITH YOUR FAMILY...

Your ideal abundant week:
With your favorite family members...

Date: _____

 WHAT ARE 3 WAYS THAT YOUR FAMILY SHARES LOVING ABUNDANCE?

1 _____
2 _____
3 _____

CELEBRATE THE CONNECTION TO YOUR FAMILY WITH 6 AFFIRMATIONS...

1 _____
2 _____
3 _____
4 _____
5 _____
6 _____

Scratch pad area...

Date:

LIST SOME THINGS YOU ARE SUPER GRATEFUL FOR TODAY!

ABUNDANCE LOG:
NOTE DOWN EVERYTHING YOU RECEIVED TODAY!

"When you want something, all the universe conspires in helping you to achieve it."

Paulo Coelho

15

Today, we are revisiting Abundance as a thankful state of being.

Fostering this state of gratitude expands into a highly attractive energy.

This energy combined with your focus on what you want, blends expansion with attraction to encompass the mental, emotional and physical manifestations of Abundance.

Abundance as wealth can be very much part of your future. Wealth can be rich experiences, spiritual wealth...and material enjoyment. It's all good!

Today's theme is based on future BE-ing.

9 MINUTES OF ABUNDANCE SCRIPTING: YOUR WEALTH AND MONEY GOALS...

Your ideal abundant month:

Envision what your wealthy Life looks like to you...

Date: _____

IDENTIFY 3 TYPES OF WEALTH YOU INTEND TO ATTRACT...

1. _____
2. _____
3. _____

WRITE 6 AFFIRMATIONS REGARDING YOUR WEALTH INTENTIONS...

1. _____
2. _____
3. _____
4. _____
5. _____
6. _____

Scratch pad area...

Date

LIST SOME THINGS YOU ARE SUPER GRATEFUL FOR TODAY!

ABUNDANCE LOG:
NOTE DOWN EVERYTHING YOU RECEIVED TODAY!

"Plant seeds of happiness, hope, success, and love; it will all come back to you in abundance. This is the law of nature."

Steve Maraboli

16

Today, we revisit the flow of Abundance.

When you allow yourself to receive as generously as you give, you affirm an abundant Self and the natural worthiness of your being.

Allow yourself to graciously accept a compliment, a gift, a kindness or an act of love and caring. Allow yourself to receive material delights too.

Today's theme is based on the Flow of receiving.

9 MINUTES OF ABUNDANCE SCRIPTING: JOURNAL OUT ANY BLOCKS AROUND RECEIVING...

Your ideal abundant month:
Receiving wealth in all its forms...

Date: _____

 ## WHICH 3 FORMS OF ABUNDANCE ARE YOU READY TO RECEIVE?

1. *Mind:* _____

2. *Body:* _____

3. *Spirit:* _____

CREATE 6 AFFIRMATIONS AROUND HOW YOU JOYFULLY RECEIVE ABUNDANCE...

1. _____
2. _____
3. _____
4. _____
5. _____
6. _____

Scratch pad area...

Date:

LIST SOME THINGS YOU ARE SUPER GRATEFUL FOR TODAY!

ABUNDANCE LOG:
NOTE DOWN EVERYTHING YOU RECEIVED TODAY!

"The universe is abundant and supports each of us. In order to see this, though, we must open all of our senses."

Thomas Lloyd Qualls

17

Today, we revisit the practice of making space for Abundance to grow.

To enjoy abundance, we need to make room emotionally. This is not to say that we should override our emotions as they arise. All emotions are valid and necessary.

Simply ensure that each day you allow yourself to fully experience all the happiness and joy that Abundance brings.

Today's theme is based on creating Space in the emotional sphere.

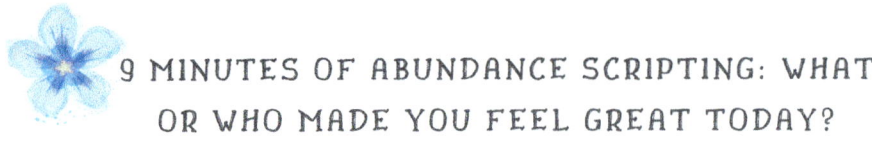 9 MINUTES OF ABUNDANCE SCRIPTING: WHAT OR WHO MADE YOU FEEL GREAT TODAY?

Your ideal abundant month:
Wealth as happy experiences...

Date: _____

WHICH 3 LOVELY ABUNDANT EMOTIONS DO YOU INTEND TO FEEL TODAY?

1. _____
2. _____
3. _____

AFFIRM 6 POSITIVE EMOTIONS YOU FEEL WHEN YOU RECEIVE ABUNDANCE...

1. _____
2. _____
3. _____
4. _____
5. _____
6. _____

Scratch pad area...

Date: _____

LIST SOME THINGS YOU ARE SUPER GRATEFUL FOR TODAY!

_____
_____
_____
_____
_____
_____
_____

ABUNDANCE LOG:
NOTE DOWN EVERYTHING YOU RECEIVED TODAY!

_____
_____
_____
_____
_____
_____
_____
_____
_____

"This is a wonderful day
I have never seen this
one before."

Maya Angelou

18

Your intentions influence every aspect of your Life. What you intend to be, do and have, can change through time.

Blending presence with intention allows you to craft your Life the way you desire.

Today's theme is based on conscious intentional Presence.

9 MINUTES OF ABUNDANCE SCRIPTING: YOUR INTENTIONS FOR THIS MONTH...

Your ideal abundant month:

Date: _____

 WRITE 3 ABUNDANT DESIRES THAT STRETCH
YOUR IDEA OF WHAT IS POSSIBLE...

1 _____

2 _____

3 _____

PUT THESE INTENTIONS INTO 6
PRESENT-DAY AFFIRMATIONS...

1 _____

2 _____

3 _____

4 _____

5 _____

6 _____

Scratch pad area...

Date:

LIST SOME THINGS YOU ARE SUPER
GRATEFUL FOR TODAY!

_____
_____
_____
_____
_____
_____
_____

ABUNDANCE LOG:
NOTE DOWN EVERYTHING YOU RECEIVED TODAY!

_____
_____
_____
_____
_____
_____
_____
_____

"Why are you so enchanted by this world, when a mine of gold lies within you?"

RUMI

19

Today, we revisit the feelings of freedom that rests at the core of Abundance.

In order to create freedom of the spirit, we must look within.

Today's theme is based on Freedom of your spirit.

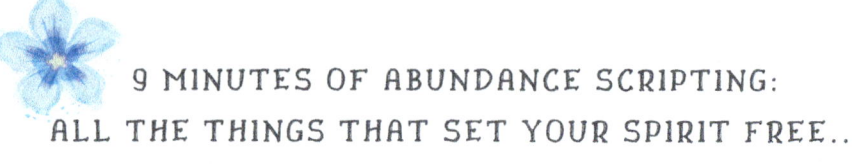

9 MINUTES OF ABUNDANCE SCRIPTING:
ALL THE THINGS THAT SET YOUR SPIRIT FREE...

Your ideal abundant month:
Things you would love to do...

Date: _____

 TODAY, DO 3 THINGS THAT MAKE YOUR SPIRIT SOAR!

1 _____

2 _____

3 _____

EXPRESS YOUR JOYFULLY ABUNDANT SPIRIT IN 6 AFFIRMATIONS...

1 _____

2 _____

3 _____

4 _____

5 _____

6 _____

Scratch pad area...

Date:

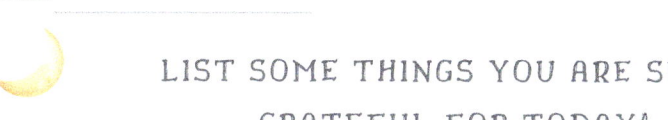

LIST SOME THINGS YOU ARE SUPER
GRATEFUL FOR TODAY!

ABUNDANCE LOG:
NOTE DOWN EVERYTHING YOU RECEIVED TODAY!

"Happiness is when what you think, what you say, and what you do are in harmony."

Gandhi

Today we revisit the beautiful energies of Abundance.

Your acceptance of the flow of Life builds contentment and happiness.

Today's theme is based on the Abundant Energy of happiness.

9 MINUTES OF ABUNDANCE SCRIPTING: HOW YOU EXPRESS YOUR HAPPINESS...

Your ideal abundant month:

Doodle things that make you happy!

Date: _____

 WHAT 3 THINGS MAKE YOU FEEL HAPPY IN MIND, BODY AND SPIRIT?

1. Mind: _____

2. Body: _____

3. Spirit: _____

WRITE 6 AFFIRMATIONS CELEBRATING THINGS THAT MAKE YOU HAPPY...

1. _____

2. _____

3. _____

4. _____

5. _____

6. _____

Scratch pad area...

Date:

LIST SOME THINGS YOU ARE SUPER GRATEFUL FOR TODAY!

ABUNDANCE LOG:
NOTE DOWN EVERYTHING YOU RECEIVED TODAY!

"Life was meant for good friends and great adventures."

UNKNOWN

21

Today we revisit the Abundant state of enjoyment.

Let's celebrate delightful experiences with good friends. And cheers to new ones!

Today's theme is based on the Enjoyment of friendship.

9 MINUTES OF ABUNDANCE SCRIPTING: JOYFUL EXPERIENCES YOU'VE HAD WITH YOUR FRIENDS...

Your ideal abundant month:
More things you'd love to experience with good friends!

Date: _____

WHAT ARE 3 FAVORITE FUN MEMORIES WTH FRIENDS?

1 _____

2 _____

3 _____

AFFIRM THAT YOU ALREADY HAVE 6 OF THE HIGHEST QUALITIES OF FRIENDSHIP...

1 _____

2 _____

3 _____

4 _____

5 _____

6 _____

Scratch pad area...

Date:

LIST SOME THINGS YOU ARE SUPER GRATEFUL FOR TODAY!

_____
_____
_____
_____
_____
_____
_____

ABUNDANCE LOG:
NOTE DOWN EVERYTHING YOU RECEIVED TODAY!

_____
_____
_____
_____
_____
_____
_____
_____
_____

"Aim for the moon. If you miss, you may hit a star."

W. Clement Stone

22

Today, we are revisiting Abundance as an expansive state of being.

An expansive state allows you to reach beyond the personal and familiar into the rich interconnectedness of the Universe.

Meditation, affirmations, laughter, music, yoga, prayer and visualization are a few ways to experience this expansive state.

Today's theme is based on expansive BE-ing.

# 9 MINUTES OF ABUNDANCE SCRIPTING: YOUR EXPERIENCE TODAY WITH ALL THAT MADE YOU FEEL EXPANSIVE...

Your ideal abundant year:
Dream it up and let it fly!

Date: _____

 WHICH 3 EXPANSIVE PRACTICES ARE
YOU EXCITED TO DO TODAY?

1 _____

2 _____

3 _____

COMMIT TO THESE EXPANSIVE
PRACTICES IN 6 AFFIRMATIONS...

1 _____

2 _____

3 _____

4 _____

5 _____

6 _____

Scratch pad area...

Date:

ABUNDANCE LOG:
NOTE DOWN EVERYTHING YOU RECEIVED TODAY!

"Abundance is not the result of unlimited opportunities or resources. It is manifested by limitless thinking, a courageous spirit, and a grateful, receptive heart."

Anthon St. Maarten

23

Today, we revisit the flow of Abundance.

All we encounter through the flow of Life creates countless learning experiences.

Some lessons are the expression of general life wisdom, while other lessons are valuable for specific areas of our lives.

Today's theme is based on the Flow of learning.

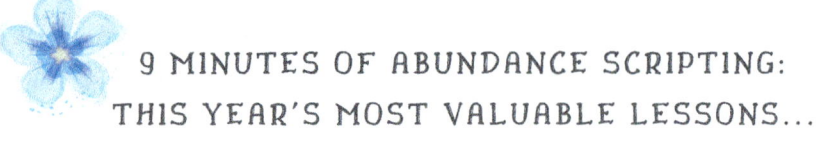

9 MINUTES OF ABUNDANCE SCRIPTING: THIS YEAR'S MOST VALUABLE LESSONS...

Your ideal abundant year:
Things you would love to learn...

Date: _____

 WHAT ARE 3 LEARNING OPPORTUNITIES
YOU'RE LOOKING FORWARD TO THIS WEEK?

1 _____
2 _____
3 _____

CREATE 6 AFFIRMATIONS EXPRESSING
YOUR OPENNESS TO LEARNING...

1 _____
2 _____
3 _____
4 _____
5 _____
6 _____

Scratch pad area...

Date:

LIST SOME THINGS YOU ARE SUPER GRATEFUL FOR TODAY!

ABUNDANCE LOG:
NOTE DOWN EVERYTHING YOU RECEIVED TODAY!

"Wear gratitude like a cloak and it will feed every corner of your life."

RUMI

24

Today, we revisit the practice of making space for Abundance to grow.

Earlier we explored freedom for your spirit. Today is about creating more space for your spirit.
This could mean allocating time for spirituality, self-love and self-esteem practices. As well, gently let go of beliefs you have outgrown.

Today's theme is based on creating Space in the spiritual sphere.

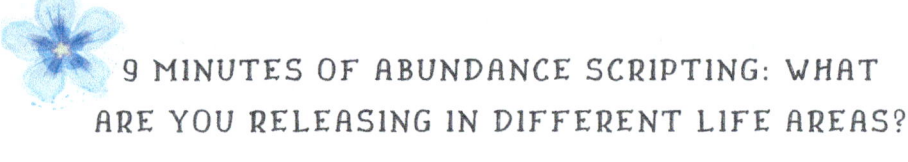

9 MINUTES OF ABUNDANCE SCRIPTING: WHAT ARE YOU RELEASING IN DIFFERENT LIFE AREAS?

Your ideal abundant year:
Food for your spirit...

Date: _____

 ## WHICH 3 SPIRITUAL PRACTICES WILL YOU ENJOY TODAY?

1. _____
2. _____
3. _____

AFFIRM 6 WAYS YOUR FAVOURITE SPIRITUAL PRACTICES IMPACT YOU...

1. _____
2. _____
3. _____
4. _____
5. _____
6. _____

Scratch pad area...

Date:

LIST SOME THINGS YOU ARE SUPER
GRATEFUL FOR TODAY!

ABUNDANCE LOG:
NOTE DOWN EVERYTHING YOU RECEIVED TODAY!

"Abundance is not something we acquire. It is something we tune into."

WAYNE DYER

25

Being mindfully present with what we learn in Life creates a rich memory bank of experiences.

Today's theme is based on Presence in learning.

 9 MINUTES OF ABUNDANCE SCRIPTING:
THIS WEEK'S LESSONS...

Your ideal abundant year:
Anything goes...

Date: _____

WHICH 3 THINGS WOULD YOU LIKE TO IMPROVE IN YOUR LIFE?

1 _____

2 _____

3 _____

COMMIT TO THESE WITH 6 AFFIRMATIONS...

1 _____

2 _____

3 _____

4 _____

5 _____

6 _____

Scratch pad area...

Date: _____

LIST SOME THINGS YOU ARE SUPER
GRATEFUL FOR TODAY!

_____
_____
_____
_____
_____
_____
_____

ABUNDANCE LOG:
NOTE DOWN EVERYTHING YOU RECEIVED TODAY!

_____
_____
_____
_____
_____
_____
_____

"Create a vision for the life you really want and then work relentlessly towards making it a reality."

Roy T. Bennett

Today, we revisit the expression of freedom that dances with Abundance.

In order to create an abundant life and future, you must be free to create your own personal vision of this.

Today's theme is based on Freedom of your vision.

9 MINUTES OF ABUNDANCE SCRIPTING:
YOUR GRAND VISION FOR LIFE ACHIEVEMENTS...

Your ideal abundant year:
Living your vision...

Date: _____

☀ LIST THREE GOALS OR DREAMS YOU DON'T WANT TO LET GO OF, NO MATTER WHAT...

1. _____
2. _____
3. _____

CREATE 6 AFFIRMATIONS THAT CONFIRM YOUR COMMITMENT TO THESE...

1. _____
2. _____
3. _____
4. _____
5. _____
6. _____

Scratch pad area...

Date: _____

LIST SOME THINGS YOU ARE SUPER GRATEFUL FOR TODAY!

_____
_____
_____
_____
_____
_____
_____

ABUNDANCE LOG:
NOTE DOWN EVERYTHING YOU RECEIVED TODAY!

_____
_____
_____
_____
_____
_____
_____
_____
_____

"You must find a place inside yourself where nothing is impossible."

DEEPAK CHOPRA

27

Today we revisit the beautiful energies of Abundance.

When painful past experiences with money (or any aspect of Life) are accepted, learned from and released, you receive fresh vitality with the beautiful energy of hope.

Today's theme is based on the Abundant Energy of hope.

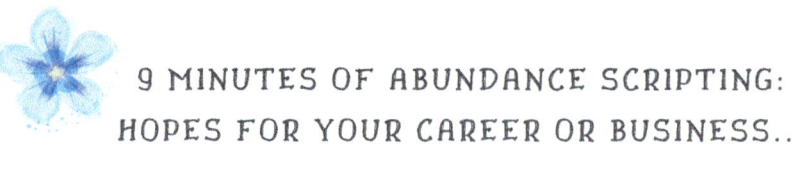

9 MINUTES OF ABUNDANCE SCRIPTING: HOPES FOR YOUR CAREER OR BUSINESS...

Your ideal abundant year:
In your career or business...

Date: _____

WRITE DOWN 3 GOALS YOU ARE VERY HOPEFUL ABOUT...

1. _____
2. _____
3. _____

WRITE 6 AFFIRMATIONS THAT EXPRESS THESE AS BEING REAL NOW...

1. _____
2. _____
3. _____
4. _____
5. _____
6. _____

Scratch pad area...

Date: _____

LIST SOME THINGS YOU ARE SUPER GRATEFUL FOR TODAY!

_____
_____
_____
_____
_____
_____
_____

ABUNDANCE LOG:
NOTE DOWN EVERYTHING YOU RECEIVED TODAY!

_____
_____
_____
_____
_____
_____
_____
_____
_____
_____

"The heart that gives, gathers."

Marianne Moor

28

Today we revisit the Abundant state of enjoyment. Abundance is in a constate state of growth and expansion.

You are connecting to the world via community, the internet, travel and all other brilliant paths of communication.

Perhaps you create services, products or art to share with the world. Perhaps you lend your time and resources to world causes. The strongest connector is...Love.

Today's theme is based on the Enjoyment of world connection.

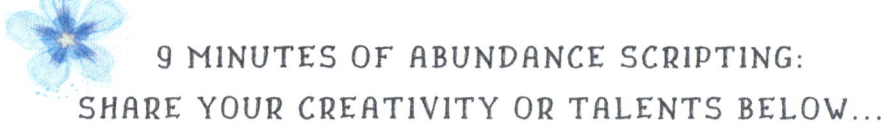
9 MINUTES OF ABUNDANCE SCRIPTING:
SHARE YOUR CREATIVITY OR TALENTS BELOW...

Your ideal abundant year:
Ways to share your beautiful Self with the world...

Date: _____

NOTE 3 IDEAS TO CONNECT
ABUNDANTLY WITH THE WORLD...

1 _____
2 _____
3 _____

CLAIM THESE IDEAS WITH 6
JUICY AFFIRMATIONS...

1 _____
2 _____
3 _____
4 _____
5 _____
6 _____

Scratch pad area...

Date: _____

LIST SOME THINGS YOU ARE SUPER GRATEFUL FOR TODAY!

_____
_____
_____
_____
_____
_____
_____

ABUNDANCE LOG:
NOTE DOWN EVERYTHING YOU RECEIVED TODAY!

_____
_____
_____
_____
_____
_____
_____
_____
_____

"Alignment is a vibration, a movement of energy that feels at once grounded, centered, and enlightened and propels you gracefully forward toward what feels good and meant for you."

Kris Franken

29

Today we revisit the beautiful energies of Abundance.

Allowing and aligning help ease you into claiming the Abundance that already exists. They draw your attention to what you're attracting and how you're expanding.

Today's theme is based on the Abundant Energies of allowing and alignment.

9 MINUTES OF ABUNDANCE SCRIPTING: OUTLINE YOUR WEALTH GOALS IN DETAIL...

Your ideal abundant year:
What you commit to aligning with this year and some of the steps you'll take...

Date: _____

WRITE DOWN 3 WEALTH GOALS YOU ALLOW YOURSELF TO REACH FOR!

1 _____

2 _____

3 _____

MAKE 6 AFFIRMATIONS THAT SHOW YOU'RE ALIGNED WITH THESE...

1 _____

2 _____

3 _____

4 _____

5 _____

6 _____

Scratch pad area...

Date: _____

LIST SOME THINGS YOU ARE SUPER GRATEFUL FOR TODAY!

_____
_____
_____
_____
_____
_____
_____

ABUNDANCE LOG:
NOTE DOWN EVERYTHING YOU RECEIVED TODAY!

_____
_____
_____
_____
_____
_____
_____
_____
_____
_____

"Action is the foundational key to all success."

PABLO PICASSO

30

Today, we revisit the flow of Abundance.

When allowing and alignment manifest into action, this lights up the path to Abundance. All it takes is one small consistent step at a time to create powerful momentum.

In spite of buzzwords such as "inspired action," actions do not always feel inspired at the time. They can often feel like hard work, but are necessary for growth.

Inspiration is created by your underlying intention, abundant energies, and vision.

Today's theme is based on the Flow of focused action.

9 MINUTES OF ABUNDANCE SCRIPTING:
PLAN MORE ACTION TOWARDS YOUR #1 GOAL...

Your ideal abundant year:
All that your heart desires...

Date: _____

THIS WEEK, WHAT 3 STEPS WILL YOU TAKE TOWARDS YOUR GOALS?

1. _____
2. _____
3. _____

CREATE 6 AFFIRMATIONS TO CLAIM MASSIVE COURAGEOUS ACTION!

1. _____
2. _____
3. _____
4. _____
5. _____
6. _____

Scratch pad area...

Date: _____

LIST SOME THINGS YOU ARE SUPER GRATEFUL FOR TODAY!

_____
_____
_____
_____
_____
_____
_____

ABUNDANCE LOG:
NOTE DOWN EVERYTHING YOU RECEIVED TODAY!

_____
_____
_____
_____
_____
_____
_____
_____
_____
_____

Amazing!

Woo Hoo!

Time to celebrate!

HOW DO YOU FEEL SO FAR?

LESSONS LEARNED AND CONTEMPLATIVE THOUGHTS...

MORE IDEAS FOR TOP GOALS... *Keep them coming!*

Notes & Doodles:

Dreams & Doodles:

What's next?

Create a year of Abundance expansion by keeping an abundance journal each month for all Life's wonders. Order a fresh journal for each month.

Plan out your wealth goals, encompassing all the joys of Life for mind, body and spirit.

And take inspired action…into the heart of Life!

Created by Joyful Life Mastery

WWW.JOYFULLIFEMASTERY.COM

Ignite
THE PATH TO A MAGICAL LIFE

Manifesting should be fun!

We know that life, change and transformation can carry their own types of growing pains.

All the more reason to make the process of transformation enjoyable.

Jump into an adventure like no other...

IGNITE: The Path to a Magical Life

Go on fun manifesting Quests, each of which will transform your life.
PLUS collect surprise manifesting gifts, trophies and badges after each Quest.

Ignite
THE PATH TO A MAGICAL LIFE

Each Joyful Life Mastery offering will give you the link to start Quest 1 for FREE. There is no obligation to continue.

However, if you decide you're ready for this adventure...

In only a few short months, your family, friends and colleagues will be amazed at the changes in your life.

But more importantly, you'll be living with a sense of poise, joyful adventure and clarity – and creating your magical life, step-by-step.

Whether you choose to sample the Joyful Life offerings a la carte or dive straight into this exciting adventure, I wish you so much inspiration, fun and happiness on your journey!

With much love,

PKDavies

Quest 1

THE COSMIC PLAYBOOK

Journey to Joy...

Daily inspiration to power your journey. Mini meditations, affirmations and intentions that spark loving mindfulness and self-awareness each day.

Visit and sign up at:

www.JoyfulLifeMastery.com

Start the Quest 1 in your adventure for FREE.

Ignite
THE PATH TO A
MAGICAL LIFE

Quest 4
JOYFUL ABUNDANCE

YOUR SECRET LINK:

https://bit.ly/3LuDVF0

MAGIC PASSWORD:

VAMmoneyscript

ignite
THE PATH TO A
MAGICAL LIFE

Visit us For More Joyful Books and Tools

www.JoyfulLifeMastery.com

www.ingramcontent.com/pod-product-compliance
Lightning Source LLC
Chambersburg PA
CBHW071432070526
44578CB00001B/81